Proof That I Was Young

Proof That I Was Young

Donald W. Crowe, MD

iUniverse, Inc.
New York Lincoln Shanghai

Proof That I Was Young

iUniverse, Inc.

For information address:
iUniverse, Inc.
2021 Pine Lake Road, Suite 100
Lincoln, NE 68512
www.iuniverse.com

ISBN: 0-595-26918-4

Printed in the United States of America

Contents

Contents

Contents

Airplane

Airplane high,
airplane low,
airplane on the ground.
May go East,
may go West,
airplane, you're the best!
(Written in Mrs. Robb's second grade.)

I write poetry because I need to. Mrs. Robb was the first outside influence that required me to capture my ideas with words. Later, however, I wrote because the ideas seemed to threaten my well being if they were not released and herded onto paper. This work represents over thirty years of ideas and my attempts to use words to preserve them.

East

The leaving is dark; I don't feel inspired.
My words are dead; I feel very tired.
I lazily watch the green float by
and wonder if you've noticed that you and I
are always saying goodbye
before our hellos have passed.
Life seems very fast.

And I remember as I fall farther away,
so many feelings I needed to say
now seem sunshine's shadows on a cloudy day.
And those things I said,
that then seemed so right,
impress me as feeble reflectors of light
 to shine as memories.

And behind me the horizon swallows
one final bite
of the evening's last light.
Its night.

And you are far away from me,
and I am far away from me
 with you.

Feelings

How can I say
what has been said so many times before
by men much smarter, but with hearts no fuller?
Why in a drained fountain of words
must all my thoughts be poured
 to spill and drop a phrases clever no more?
My great seems their feeble,
their great seems far away.
They write what I think but cannot say
 in a new and different way.
So words limp from my pen very weak,
and I am unable to say what I seek
 to tell you.
And were I to say, "I love you,"
There is nothing in these words exciting or new.
Still this is the best
I have to give.

Summer '72

Love,
Beth
ended the letter I got from you today
and now I sit and try to choose the words you'd say
if I asked "do you love me?"
I fear you'd run away.

I carefully avoided the word you used above,
it seemed somehow forbidden to use the word love
 when we were close.
It scarred us both I think.
In fact, it still scares me,
for every time I've set it free
 its changed my world around.
It seems like love and man have found
 something they can share—
they each use and destroy to progress
and neither seems to care
that taking so much power is stripping their worlds bare
 of starlight walks
 and honest talks
 and freedom.

Or perhaps I've never met love.
God, I hope that's true,
 and the imposter that I think is love

I'll keep away from you
 by burying the word so deep within my mind
 it only again shall leave me the time I find
 I've met my other half for he rest of my life—
 my wife.

So, I'll not say "I love you, Beth,"
I like you very much.
For these words are so much better
 and have a softer touch—
 like playing tennis in the rain
 and holding hands.

Birthday

Its two decades now,
since you gave my life a home—
a body, a world,
a time in which to roam.
And I've spent my time learning
how much I do not know,
between moments of laughter,
and hiding in sorrow.

I've cursed this world you gave me,
and thought about escape
from all its "real" necessities
into dreams it would have me rape.

But I've also given thanks,
to what, I do not know,
for a smile, a touch, a love,
or a chance again tomorrow.

And you, my parents,
who gave me reality,
be you guideposts, reasons,
or part of me,
twenty years ago
you gave me a place to stay.

That was gift enough
is all I mean to say.

Wish

Were I given a wish,
I would wish
to wish no more,
for wishing usurps beginning
and wrings tears from dreams.

Infinity

I look in 'till I can't see
and watch all outside engulfing me.
All above and all below
and one more number than I know.
Inquisitive "whats," unknowing "whys,"
the dark deepness of your eyes,
the sky, the sea, the color blue,
the stars, beauty, and mostly you.

I touch, merely imprint as if sand
 on an unending beach.
And I realize
all is forever, save me

Huh?

How does I feel?
Can you feel the fame?
So sorry. I'm so forgetful
you don't know that your name
is scrawled on an beach
very far away.
So how can you say?

August 3rd

My eyes lift up so I can see
a soaring gull reminding me
that your are there—
    as in all beauty.

I can see you but you aren't here,
I feel you here but you're not near,
In the silver-blue distance I see you there
I can almost reach out and touch your hair.
You're there.

You almost cried as you said goodbye.
I know the answer but I still must ask why—
if you are about me in so many ways
why must you feel as I feel so far away?
Still, a million todays are born for tomorrow
and one of these times for a while I will borrow
 and return it only after we're together.
For we still look up to the same stars
and I doubt that your travels may take you so far
that I can't reach out and touch you.

Growing

Amidst the drunkenness and cigars,
old friends and new blue cars,
picked up broads and old IU,
week-end adventures and bad follow-throughs,
the solitary walks and the fraternity,
Grouch impersonations and poetry,
the pseudo involvements and one nigh stands,
impulse voyages and very big plans,
 I'm waiting for something to want.
And once I've found it
 I know I'll start living.

Via V.C's

Your tears, so slippery
that my words tripped and fell
before they could reach your ear.
They tumbled and jumbled
and bounced back on me;
and amidst their scent of liquor
came a sound I couldn't bare—
 the truth—
that I had made you cry.

Ghost

I desire you, for you have Susan's smile.
I laugh at you, for you have Linda's comedy.
I need you, for you have Beth's goodness.
I envy you, for you have Ellen's opportunity.
I lie to you, for you have Julie's body.
I display you, for you have Bonnie's beauty.
I question you, for you have Cheryl's curiosity.
I stroke you, for you have Cindi's innocence.
I ponder you, for you have Ann's nervousness.
I touch you, for you have Ellie's warmth.
I float with you, for you have Dd's freedom.
I stumble in my blindness for I open my eyes
  and find myself alone.

On Hypocrisy

How vocal I am when I don't know
what are my feelings or how I can show
 who I am for a time.
Words without rhyme or meaning grow
in the web of my philosophy.
Words that aren't me
I stack high in a wall
 many "hypocrisies" tall
to cower behind
and use the time
to collect my thoughts, and present them as me.
But its too late—its the wall that is seen
 not me.
So I wait, locked in a cover
of words 'till they smother
each other
 and rot
to free every thought
and leave me as me
with my philosophy
 and identity
 until the next time I'm shook and start talking.

Presents

I love enough now to let you go—
  then hope you don't take my life and leave.
But if you find yourself drifting,
  pushed by a gentler wind's blow
  then go, and don't grieve
  for the part of me you take.
For no one makes too big a mistake
by giving love.
And the void in me
will fill with age and memory.

I'm giving you your freedom,
  A gift you've always had.

Woman

Spilled, lost,
that which would have sustained me,
all because I was too hurried too drink.
You promised a sweet escape
 into drunkenness
 and I was so thirsty.
Now my tears mix with you.
Soon they'll wash you away,
 and I'm with myself but very much alone.

Be Quiet While I Celebrate You

Sing your songs, new love,
 but do not speak to me.
For words would most likely suffocate
 my dreams of what you could be.

Ginny Doesn't Know How to Tell Me

How unfortunate
 that a bubble, colossal enough to
 to carry a life away,
can be broken by the flick of an eyelash
 welcoming tomorrow to today.

Good morning to reality—and I understand.

The Past Is a Lady (Was She So Beautiful)

Each minute separates us,
and as I strain to see her,
she grows more beautiful than before.
She leaves,
 only to return, invited or not,
for she knows where I am,
and how to tease me into wanting her.
But when I reach
I grasp only reality,
who she won't abide,
for it seems they'd once been close
but he had stood her up.
She leaves,
and we go on.
But she'll return soon
 more beautiful than before.

Sad

Tomorrow will be real again,
and I will smile without realizing,
and feast on laughter
 until my fullness kills its taste.
But now these are treasures
 since my thoughts of you are wide enough
to make them out of reach.

Not In Such A Long Time

It hurt,
 and the words welled up
 and rolled down my pen.
Everyone knew something was wrong.
But I kept crying—
for no one knew
 how to kiss away words.

Morning After

If you cannot smile, my love,
 look tired or look away.
But don't pierce me
 with eyes that say,
"I'm sorry."
For remorse paints love with reality,
 and tears from finding faults in the hues
 can smear and wash away a masterpiece.

Clock

My love has gone,
 and now I plead for you to speak.
But your silence gives no forgiving
for my curses thrown before,
 when your shouts grew louder than love.

Tell me that this hour's done
since she won't return before you command,
and I must know we're closer.

The only comfort is with eyes closed
as you beat me with unmoving hands,
 so I'll sleep until you awaken me.

Games

My eyes screamed in deafening silence
a demand for your promise of love.
But you just smiled a whisper
I couldn't understand.
Now, I could wait no longer
so I said the words first;
and again, I settle for
an "I love you, too."
I'll be back soon
   for that light too quickly dims
   and I'm afraid of the dark.
But you know that,
   don't you, my love.

Informed?

There are pictures
of war and princesses
 and places I've only heard of.
Worldwide, tremendous, essential—
the words are like balloons,
floating large, yet empty,
 lighting softly on my brow.
Soon they will hide
where they're from.
I cannot understand
how knowing these
will make the sun rise more skillfully.
The late-night news? Bah!
They never even told me
what your dreaming of now,
 as you lay beside me.

Moods

I'm on the brink of loneliness;
I know I'm about to fall.
And even if thousands were to hear me cry,
they'd bring no solace at all.
I know so little of my life,
I just inhabit its passing seasons.
And I feel now an autumn retreating
to leave cold as its wake—not reasons.
So I'll stumble into winter
because its time for it once more,
and the search to find what brings the change
will show only I'm as blind as before.
My moods can turn the world around,
 and doom me to fall like hourglass sand.
But this fate seems more just somehow,
 when I feel you take my hand.

October

This autumn day
grants divinity with an unseen wind,
gives strength with fulfilling cold,
and the knowledge allowed me
 by nature's artistry,
Tells me, for now, I'm not becoming old.

I could crush this stone
 if I needed to impress,
Or could fly anywhere,
 if I needed to go.
But for now, on this day
I think I'll just stay—
I don't need to search "why?'
 I know.

No Poetry

When I looked back at the dusk
because it was beautiful,
the guilt I felt for looking
away from your eyes,
robbed me of my love for you both.
And I almost lost myself
 as I gave chase.
I can no longer hide within your radiance—
your humanness has too much dimmed the glow.
How sad I was to find you're a woman.
I was a fool who would have the sunset stay,
and who feared the dark when it came.

I awoke in a dawn
 that celebrated yesterday's passing.
And as I watched
I held you
and loved you both.

Music Box

Now the music plays again.
It confuses and it understands
and the sound is touch to an opened hand.

It's time to say, "I love you,"
because the sun has come to give us day
 and a taste of life in which to play
while we wait for limitless night.

How easily the melody holds thoughts in flight,
as now the music plays again.
It asks questions and it replies
and the sound is sight with closed eyes.

Its time to say, "I'll not leave,"
for there's a sunset coming, I believe
 and within its grasp it holds the night
and darkness to dream in as we wait for light.

How easily the melody holds thoughts in flight
as now the music plays again.
It makes no demands, but hears no appeals
and the sound is life if it's free to be real.

It's time to say, "I love you."

Saturday Morning Before 11:00

I only want to live and die.
 I cannot settle for half of this.

Dancing

You keep smiling at me.
 And I wonder if it's because
I remember that you smiled when I left.
Or maybe because
 I know that you smile most always.
Or maybe because
 I really see you when my thoughts turn your way.

The Mirror Is Steamed Up

I've noticed
 that I shave quite often,
but if you put a squirt gun in my hand,
 you're liable to get wet.
How can I know if I'm a man?

Listening To What I Cannot Hear

You cry to be free
  but with every thrust reach no farther than before.
Except that you tear farther into me
  when I walk across your besieged shore.

I wonder how what I think and feel
  will help the sun shine tomorrow,
or make your touch more real
  than the dream of impending love I now know.

The fire of imagined tomorrow, I sit by to keep warm
  burns me when I stare from too near—
But you simply wash it away with the tides shapeless form
As if to say, "tomorrow is already here."

Transition

When I cast a stone into the sea
 I know it will be returned to me
 in a thousand years or so.
And it comforts me greatly to know
that this will always be true.
It frees my mind to think of you
and how I'll love you when we meet
 and how we'll find together that the sky is blue
 and raindrops taste so sweet.

Now The Tide Has Come

The only things real
are the wetness I feel
 and the life near enough to see.
Before me another world calls—each wave beckons me
to forget that behind me, and not too far
is my own world waiting there.
I can't hear what the sea's promises are
 But of this morning at least I don't really care.

Tears For A Rape

If you listen too long to the songs of the sea,
these sounds will be your final melody.
If you watch the sun rise to long into day,
for debasing this beauty, your sight you must pay.
If you bid your love make you smile too much
you'll kill the softness in her touch.

Please listen—although I still hear and see
I have no one left to make me happy.

Morning Winds

A wave that whitecaps far away
  and draws to it your eyes,
Very seldom reaches the shore
  before it quiets and dies.

Correspondence #3

It's a revolution.
What I'm trying to be
endeavoring to capture me.
I'm on the former's side,
but we're at a disadvantage,
for poets don't make good fighters.
The pen that prods and starts the fight
 makes an awfully dull sword,
and one needs a weapon of substance
 when the opposition is not concerned
 with words or explanations or poems—
 only winning.
And this enemy calls on his ally, the body
 to give him the most unaesthetic weapons,
so decisive
that they dissolve the desire for victory into bliss.

Couldn't you see that there was a war going on?
No, I guess you didn't know me well enough to hear the battle.
I needed a peacemaker,
but I found you, a prize to fight over.
And I did fight—not for, but over you,
like a battlefield.
I scarred you

with every siege and retreat.
And the coup d etat failed this time, anyway.

I'm sorry.
 I wish I could cry for you,
but soldiers can't regret
 for then they wouldn't learn and become wise.
And unwise soldies
are always defeated
 until they die.

It Meant Something Once

Why must I always want
  what can't be had until it's given.
For a taker, it's such a long wait
  that I fear my life is wasting—
all my efforts are no better than hope.

All I want is to make you happy.
More than anything else,
  I want to see you smile.

Wednesday

I was strong when I held you.
 And if you'd asked why the sky was blue,
 a poet I would have become.
You looked at me and made me handsome.
Your questions seemed to make me wise,
and your listening made honest the lies
 that too often usurp what is me.
When you said, "yes," I found I was free,
 and your smile took me farther,
It made me happy.

Not Hurt Alone

She's gone,
and everything now
seems so important.
I'm very aware of my role—
I think that the author has come
to see the performance,
  and I do so want to star.
A tragedy depends on its lead,
  you know,
    to make it all seem real.

Telephone

You say, "Hello."
I start to die.
I hear no other sounds
  but feel you say goodbye.

Drunkard

In a few minutes
 I'll close my eyes,
 and wait for another morning.
And I'll have made it through a day
 without you.
But there'll be no celebrating this victory.

Tenth Street

You might be right,
 and I may never pick up
 any women.
But it's natural for me
 to walk north
 with one foot pointed East
 and the other West.
And I'll not change what's me.

I'm Glad I Found You

You were warm on a cold night
and it felt right
to be there
and aware
that it was good—
even though it hurt
for the numb
to go
and show
how cold I was.
And when the warm was done,
I felt no want to run
away from there,
but I left
because it was time
to go
and so
cold came
and some pain
before the numb again.

Sleeping Dreams

He never saw the sunset, so he couldn't claim the day
  as being part of his life—life passed too far away.
He never worked 'till sundown, the dusk he found so cold,
  he shut his eyes to the painted sky, the reason to get old.

His life was just existing, too frightened too begin,
  and his greatest pride was remembering his worlds that might
    have been.
His sleep ended the yesterday he was ready for today,
  and all day long he watched the birds while on the grass he lay.

They flew high and near the sun
so far from his life's prison.
And the music in each soft free wing
was the only song he tried to sing.

So many loves would be making life had someone said "Hello,"
but sleeping dreams are easier than the dreams this day can
    know.
If the first step won't be made then the journey isn't new,
and there is no good in living dreams if the dreams cannot be
    true.

His tears and he both hit the ground when he tried to join their
    flight,
  and as the flew around the sun his eyes flew into night.

He never saw that sunset or another day begin,
he died because he realized this life had never been.

Saturday 1

Time is nothing more
  than the darkness guarding dreams.

Saturday 2

I am what I am
  to lure what I want.
But what I want will only come
  to what is really me.
I'm dizzy from the circles.

Saturday 3

What is believed is real.
What is real never dies.

Hookey From Life

Of all the lessons I've never learned,
 the lesson I've never learned most often
is that I can't make you feel.
In fact, I'm not learning it again
 every time I try to appeal
to the miser who invests your smiles.

I Know Frustration

God, let me love you,
then everything will be alright.
 And I won't be searching every night
for anything that says, "I'm new,
 and can't be had by you."

Numb

I met a girl In a meeting
 and spent the hour
 deciding if she was pretty.
But I didn't know you then.

I hustled a girl in a parking lot
 and my ego won a kiss.
But I didn't know you then.

I loved a girl with a bottle of wine.
But I didn't know you then.

I cry as you say goodbye
for I never knew you.

Alike Without Harmony

The most beautiful woman
 I've never know
is anyone
 who wouldn't be with me tonight.

Make Me Stop Asking

I'll love you
 until I understand why.

Taxes

Love:
How sad that we pay
 So high a price
For that which is free.

Second To Last

What might have been
  was not, and never will it be.
In this there is no good or bad,
  No randomness, no destiny.
And most of all no poetry.

Only Maybe

I only want someone not to be lonely with,
 for I know you can never keep me happy.
If you make me happy
 that's enough to love you for,
since I can do neither.

Anonymous

There are times I wonder if my years were spent
 missing you,
before I knew who
 you were.

I don't know why I need you,
I just feel that I do.
Perhaps your face reflects to me
 a world without question to infect its beauty.
Or maybe your eyes and the answers they give
 make it simpler to live with the questions.
Or maybe times and places make the moments of my life
 and you just chanced to share them.
I don't know.

It seems you make life easier.
that's enough.

Mother

I can't understand how you held on to me
when I fought so very hard to be free.
But you knew enough to make me grow,
and now I must tell you what you already know—
  you are much of what is me.

In everything good I ever do,
please hear me saying I care for you,
for I'm too dumb to say
  "I love you" in any other way.

Father

I never knew you father,
 until you were a friend.
You were a loud voice, security,
 and rules that wouldn't bend.
But I never saw a person there,
 I never really tried.
It was enough to have you near
 to reinforce my pride.

Now I'm older and I'm changed somehow.
It might be that I don't fear you now.
For I see myself when I see you
 and I understand what you've gone through
 to be a dad to me.

When I see you now I see a man—
a man who has done all he can
 to be a father to me.
And I respect you.

For Selfishness

I loved you for you made me love myself,
for I knew no words or luck or wealth
could make you stop looking for awhile.
I knew that I would have to make you smile.

Since what was me would make you stay
 or displease you enough to go away
 and search elsewhere,
I began to care
about the kind of man you'd see
 if you stopped so you could look at me.
The bad in me I took to hide
 and filled its place with quiet pride
 in what was good.

So I became the man I want to be—
and when you were with me,
 I loved myself as I loved you.

Now I fear you love me too much,
for in each unasked for touch
 you say you care for all of me.
 And my best I need not be to keep you.

The love for me is dying
for myself I'm no longer trying

to be—
I know you'll love me anyway.

On Life #1

Once, when I was high on happy,
I took a look below me
and the world
unfurled.

And I felt very lucky
that it was given to me,
for given it must have been,
 for I never worked or had to win
 a qualifying round.
I just found
 this life when I opened my eyes.

On Life #2

People are too free
when they can't see
life was given
where nothing was before.
And they have no right
to be here,
they just are.

On Life #3

In life you can't lose
for no one lets you choose.
So you can't be wrong
whichever way you go.

Up, Via Wonder

When I'm lost in me
I look down and see
that I can feel my pen
and move it when
I want to.
So I think on this awhile
and smile,
when I realize,
I can think too.

There Is No Wasted Time

Don't mourn flowers that never grew.
Instead be happy that you knew
the beauty you found
while looking around
for beauty
that wasn't to be.

After Atheists

I'd rather have no explanation of love
than to hear that the feeling above
is a bunch of nerve impulses.
For this paints a scientifically tangible façade
that repulses me
since it hides the only God
I've known—
the smiles you've shown
to me,
and the reasons I can't see
behind them.

Twenty Minutes

What I feel, I've never felt before,
but I have almost.
It's not a different island I explore,
it's just a different coast.

Listen, Hear

The color of love
is never new.
It simply comes
in different you's

Original

I used to write poetry on paper towels,
  so I'd known the proof of my thoughts was dying.
For I knew what I felt, like dusk to end the day,
would inspire me before it faded away,
and in this darkness if I were made to say
I felt now what I felt before,
  I'd be lying.

I used to write poetry on paper towels.
But now I see that feelings that prowl
my entangled soul are the ones that fly
from one place and time
to a different now—that rhymes
and is only slightly new.

Now I keep what I write
for climbing upon them might
give me a look at what I'm feeling.

Doctrine Of An Atheist, From A Used Blue Envelope

I.   She

Perhaps I should just be your friend
and not want you to lend
me what is you,
to find if we two
have answers to share.
Or at least to find if you'd care
to hunt them together.

II.   She and I

Perhaps we were meant to be only as real
as the laughter, tears, or warmth that I feel
if my skin brushes yours.
Maybe the "why's" behind these, where I hunt for reality,
only exist in me
and were never meant to be
anything more than fool's gold
for those whose blindness makes them bold
enough to reach for its shine.

III.   Reality

Perhaps I'm wrong in searching reasons
for what **is** so blatantly.

Perhaps the change of the seasons
should only inspire me
to think the earth has tilted a little more,
than it was before.

IV   Reality and Me

But somehow
I'd like to see love in a flower,
and I'd like to feel that the power
tingling through me
as I hold you, and we see
the sun fall away,
is aesthetic enough not to be found on a shelf,
or in a pill I take to give myself
the same contentment with life.

V.   Differences

If you find a flower and call it a plant
then you're different then me,
and I feel sorry for you if you can't see
it can mean so much
beyond a sticky-soft-touch
and an odor.
But I suppose you feel sorry for a person who searches
for something he can't be sure is there.
I guess that's fair
although justice just isn't involved.

VI   Friends

So friend, if you only want to give me
what you say and what you let me see

on the outside,
I will understand
and try to learn from us
which of us is right.

Homecoming I.

Tomorrow you'll have a face I can touch,
and the eyes that are so much
for a half-blind transient
will be close enough to let me see myself.
And I'll see I'm so much better than I thought,
but want to be much more.

Homecoming II.

Tomorrow you'll have a face
  and a smile to give me, if I please you.
Tomorrow you'll have a voice
  and the intoxicatingly wrong words to upset my strategy.
Tomorrow you'll have a hand
  and a squeeze to give mine when I say I care.

Tomorrow you'll be you—
instead of the reason for me,
  until we are once again.

Resolution: Only Freedom Illuminates Love

If you walk through a different garden
I won't try to stop you,
for your love I'd never win
if you thought someone new
 could give you more.
Even now I might love someone who
gives me what I felt before
 when I hoped you and I were near.
I still remember you made me smile so much
and I have the most hungry fear
that if you go, I'll have lost the softest touch
 that ever braved my skin.
Still, if you see a shinier light, I know you'll leave
and try to find someone who wants to begin;
and I'll smile, but I will grieve
 at my having lost you.

Does Anyone Feel This Way?

Am I me
or what I'm trying to be.

At least in all the people I've found
while living around
for eighteen years
I've narrowed it to two, here
that could be what I am.

Between the two,
what I feel
and what I do,
I'm caught in a war.
Errant shells tore
 my peace away
 the day
I began to sink
into malcontent,
knowing there was something I didn't have
to match all I'd been given.

Between me
and what I'm trying to be,
 I can't say who'll win.
 And when they begin
again to square and fight

I won't even know which side is right
to be on.
My mind is an ally of what I should be
and in my poems and lonely times they're free
to plan their attack
  and devise schemes to sack
the temple of what I am.
But my body and doings are entrenched in me
(the me that people see when I stop talking of what I will be)
and they feel quite secure
  and content to lure
  their attackers onto home ground
where they have found
in battles before
  the enemy can't ignore
the good feelings in the home crowd
  shouting so loud
one can't remember why to fight–
a terrible plight
for a soldier,
but it's sure
  the opposition has twice as many more
it creates to continue the war.

I know those who survive
thrive
in conflict.
  But I wish a stop would be picked
from all the going,
so I could start again and feel my direction

and connection
 with life.

I don't think I'm asking for peace,
just for love to bring a truce

Expendable Demands #2

Why are we the most damned of your creation?
Why, God, did you curse us so?
Have we offended you?
Are we a mistake?
Or are we simply meant to be different
to complete some plan?
God, why have you left our being—
and left in your void most pungent malcontent?
Why was it only we, the humans
 that you cursed with the ability to reason
and ask "why," and then hope for an answer?
Are we always to search for something you've hidden too well?
Are we always to be slaves of our fear
 while all about us are content to be?
Must we always build explanations of You
in human form, where we are divine and above all
 save you,
 even though our reason
shows us the hell we make for ourselves in such inconsistencies?
Is this hell, perhaps,
 this sea of malcontent in which You've doomed us to drift?

I suppose all I really want is for You
 To let me not ask so may questions.

Too Simple

I can't see
how beauty can be
anything more than believing
in your being
 and living.

Plagiarism

Come on world, inspire me.
 Don't you see,
 I'm ready to write poetry?
I'm giving the time,
you just give me the rhyme,
 and we'll make something new,
just me and you.

One thing more
 on this beauty we've bore,
I'll put my name
 and take the fame.
If you mind simply say so.
I can't hear anything, I guess that means no—
 you don't mind.
You're a good sport.

Logic

If I never loved,
 I wouldn't be hurt,
for I'd never feel

If I never loved,
 I wouldn't need to try,
for I'd never learn

If I never loved,
 I could always be as I am,
for I'd never grow.

If I never loved,
 I wouldn't need poems
for I'd never take time to see.

But if I was never to love
 I couldn't have found you,
but I already did,
 so I do.

Sleep, I'm Sure Is More Healthful

When all the smiles have faded away
 I see only one reason for living this day—
that I might be with you again.

And waiting days seem full of rain
that makes me cold
 when my thoughts are so bold
to wonder if you feel the same.

Victory

I never said I'd love you forever,
 for I'm very clever
in war games.
And to promise you
would be the same
as admitting that you've won—
and with all the fighting done
you might go,
as I have before.

I'm Not Until You

I never looked for answers until you asked why.
I saw no sunsets before I felt you sigh—
and now you say the day is through,
 but this makes me smile for tomorrow, too,
 I might be with you.
And when I touch the hand you give,
 I know I live.

You make me live my life to fast,
fleeing the fear each moment might be our last,
and making me want to start another
 before the first has passed.

By Don Crowe

With a half-chewed pen
 and some notebook pages
i think of some words
that can be remembered for ages,
 and with them my name.

Why can't i be happy with me,
 instead of finding words with a different rhyme
that no one needs or wants to take time
 in hearing.

Must everyone know
of don crowe
i think not.
But why then this poem.

My God, i'm screwed up at times.

Trio (For Now)

None of us know where we're going,
 but friends are landmarks along the way.

None of us know where we're going,
 but freedom lights our path.

None of us know where we're going,
but happiness, for a time, tells us where we are.

Trio #2

Call the man who believes in nothing
 a foolish man.
Call the man who believes in what's real
 a frustrated man.
Call the man who believes in what makes him happy
 a wise man.

Our only purpose is to find happiness,
for only in this reflection
 can we see we're alive.

I always hear the birds sing,
 but when I'm with you,
 I find myself listening.

Cooling It

I suddenly thought that you might no love me,
and I fell very deep
in a hole where escape was only a leap,
  but I had no legs.
I found myself half of nothing,
in a hole with no way out—
  a dark pit of doubt.

I felt your caring,
and the hole broke about me.
Light came and I could see
that you are as the sky,
to accept as beauty and not ask why,
  to find an unanswered answer that can't be understood.

Through the clouds of doubt I see
  that I only rule half of you and me.
And I can only watch you go or stay,
  for not the cleverest words I say
can make you mine and not yourself.
There's nothing I can do
  but care for you.

I Can't Understand How You Made The Leaves

When next I see a flower
 I'll think of you
and wonder if you're second cousins
 twice removed,
 or something.
More likely
 your daughters of the same life.
So beautiful
and real.
Neither of you
trying to be someone else.
Both of you living
and in the being
giving beauty
 to all who pass by.
 And while I looked,
when I stopped to look,
you gave me a purpose
for living some more,
A purpose so happy
 that I knew
 but couldn't understand.
And a purpose
 for what I'd already lived.
 And this made me smile

and hold you tighter.
I'm sorry I can't thank you
well enough for the life.
But in the smile you made
is a thank you
For making me smile.

Those Who Shout Loudest Are Hardest To Hear

Take me.
Can't you see
in all the poetry
I'm trying to be heard.
In every word
there's a plea
from what I want to be
to be set free
 by you.
For from two
grow one.
And if my growing can't be done
so I can see
 what I want to be
 in me
 maybe
 I can find what I want to be
 in us.

For One Who Wouldn't Kiss Back

For the one I tried to impress
who gave me the feeling she couldn't care less,
thank you for letting me see
 so much of me.
I was so many people when I was with you
 hoping that if you saw someone new
you might stop and look.
I was really shook
when you walked by.

But the shaking did me good, I'm sure
for happiness I was trying to lure
 and not befriend—
 and in the end
if I make you smile and the I isn't me,
not much sharing would there be—
in fact, there'd be none at all.

I knew this once, but I forgot,
and I really feel I owe you a lot
 for reminding me.
I hope you can see
that **I** am thanking you.

For Your Birthday

You leave me too few words to say
and its very hard to find a way
  to make this special,
  to make you happy, well
to make you smile, anyway.

You've taken all my words
  when that which I need to say
  can only be safely heard
in an ambiguous way
  by necessity
  of strategy.
I'm in a ridiculous game
  where losing and playing are the same.
  But I play
  anyway

I can't say anything without saying too much
  and that's the reason I touch
  your hair—
to make you aware
of feelings there
that want to touch you
  without my hand.

These words look like some I've gathered before;
but I can think of nothing more
  to help me show—
  to let you know
  I want to be here again.

Losing

I wonder if it's losing you
　or losing to him
　　that is killing me most.
But I cannot have lost
　what I never had,
　　and there is no game to declare
　　victory or defeat.

There is only your love
　and my pain.

Heaven Is Hell That Can't Be Reached

I live now, since you didn't love me
to feel how wondrous my next love will be
to make thoughts of you a memory
　and not heaven made hell by reality.

You Are —Always

If you should cry
　because no one cares,
　　your tears will fall where love has died,
for there could be none left at all
　were there none touching you.

Love (Crossed Out)

It seems these times I'm alone with me
I can think far enough so I can see
 man's self and his society.

People—images scurrying by
Stopping, looking, leaving,
in a search that seems foolish
 for they seek what the are.
And in their quest for themselves they reach far
into loud and quiet,
into things and God.
And that I watch myself with them seems odd,
for hunting and testing I no longer do.
 I uncovered myself when I met you,
because as you're close to me
I fall into your eyes and see
the kind of me I seem to be.

From my pensive perch I watch the world's errant tenants,
 and you and I
 amidst, but not at all close to them.

Still Again

I wish you would bore me
 and hurt me

and make me feel guilty.
Its been two years
 since I've seen you,
and I love you again.

Turned Around

Did you have to look so pretty
  while telling me good-bye.
Or smile so inaudibly
  when you bid me, "Don't ask why?"

Before I knew you
  I wanted you very much.
But a woman is never so desired
  As when she eludes a second touch.

Time

A void.
A point.
A line.
The line is time,.
 stretched woven by a Maker
spiraling about, around, among, forming a mind.
Separating and sealing as it turns
the thoughts and moments and images called life
into transparent memories—
 changeable from without
 but not to be touched.
The line pushes on for all
piecing the darkness
creating now on the outside
and past on the inside
of an ever growing spiral,
until the end is met,
and the spiral has no more room to grow,
but turns and closes still, so light and life find no sanctuary.
And the spiral meshes into the dark void
 from which another is born.

Within That Look Away

Purity fades to nakedness,
softness becomes weight and pain.
Our embrace is now a hiding place,
as the window's song turns to rain.

I ponder what your eyes have said.
I know now love has gone.
You said, "I'm sorry," with a glance—
I'll soon be moving on.

Dancing To You

I hear you and must write a song
 for whoever made my melody
in hope that my effort can inspire Him
 to sing another verse for me.

For You

I hope you'll love me
when you read this,
 for that's what it's designed to do.
It's built to motivate a kiss
 so I can find you.

Let's Eat

I should have written last night
when my words were alive,
for then they'd revive
what I'm trying to say.

It's a shame thoughts melt away
 like snowflakes to the touch
that leaves you wondering how much
lived in the uniqueness there.
It seems unfair

that thoughts should die
the next day.

Yesterday

When I awoke to feel that beside me lay you,
I opened my eyes to a day free and new.
It was the best of times to live within
So I woke you up so I could begin.

Thought #?

Death is the cocoon
From which butterflies are born.

I Wish It Were Enough

Sometimes, I love you very much.
But sometimes I feel only
 that I could live this life with you
 and not that I must.

Later That Night

I lie here thinking I'm hungry,
or that I might be in love,
 for isn't that what they say it's like—
an emptiness and desire
 felt in one's quiet times.
It's been so long since I felt anything,
 I'm truly afraid
 to get up and fix a bowl of cereal.

Memories

Memories, like flowers,
 are best kept pressed
 between the pages of a lifetime
 to bring joy when chanced upon
 while flipping through the past.
They remain beautiful
only so long as tender and brief examinations
expose them to a present
 bent on crumbling them.

I Used You Perhaps, But Needed You More

To explain what I could only feel
to trace it with words and color it real
was an impossible task—
I'm sorry you had to ask
 what there was to join you and I.
I could only answer by saying goodbye.

If there were trust those words wouldn't be needed,
you would know I told all in touches that pleaded
 for tomorrow to be ours.

Woodswoman

The woodswoman came
 and I shook just enough to recognize your presence.
I remained stiff and proud
as you cut.
And as you left
I was still stiff and proud
 lying fallen on the ground.

I.

Beauty without love is pain
  but then,
  so is everything else.

II.

I long so much to love you,
  that I no longer love to live
  without being able to.

Apologies To A Love Without Infatuation

There's no reason not to love you,
and no reason to hunt someone new
to give my love to.
But I do.

I never know why I love or how long it will last.
I only know **that** I love and I know its passed
when I no longer feel the same—
like if your name
doesn't find me
when I 'm lost in beauty
 of all I see.

If I don't love you it's not that I don't want to.
It's simply that I don't.
And no one's to blame
although I feel some shame
in having so weak a voice
 in making the choice
of who I am to care for.
It seems the draw was made before
 I had a chance to make the seedings.

Again

In your smile, my love
you ask only that I be myself.
 And I wonder
if you like me as much
as you say,
why do you require such
 a difficult task.
At least under cover of love,
I'll be less prudish about changing
 in public.

I'm glad
you saw through my mask
of confidence
and strength,
and let me be half our arch,
 as we lean on each other.
And besides
we're better in a strong wind
than you were
 or I was.

#2

The mind
  bears as it grows, the fruit of experience
  that produce myriad seeds
  so fertile that the probing of thoughts and daydreams
  spawns the growth of a full measure
  of simple, embellished, and modified memories.
So within the garden mind grow reflections,
  for some to harvest and learn from
  for some to live in and hide in until there life rots about them,
  and the stench reaches and repulses all save the source.
Still, as surely as there remains a spring to proceed it,
  change overcomes.

Revelation On A Monday

I'm sorry that I won't be your friend
and if we should ever meet again
I won't say hello,
I won't let you know
that I need to love you,
 and need you to love me, too.

I wish I could love you without knowing your name
for if I could, wouldn't this world be the same
as a family, can't you see?
 We'd be together.

The weather is getting cold
around here,
 and I fear I'm getting old.
Here, I have to know you
before I can show you
I care.
Beware world
that mold I ain't going to fill.
And if I need to change things I will.
 Hello everybody, I just want to say
I'm not afraid to smile if you pass my way.
And if we share part of today

this time you'll here me say,
"Hello."

I hope I can find you another day,
and I pray I can believe in a way
  to know its you
  in the human zoo.
  I want to take you with me.
Can't you see you'll be free?
  A way out together.

Crumpled Paper Philosophy

1. Only a quiet belief in yourself
   can silence the screams to seek praise.

2. In this life
   the only stops are made
   to worry that you've stopped.

3. Don't search for dreams,
   for they can only be had or lost.
   Strive to keep searching,
   in this you'll find life.

4. Lonely people are those who forget
   that there are more miracles than they will ever know.

5. Perhaps this is hell:
   to know all that could be
   and believe that nothing is.

6. Reality is a crutch for existence.
   God has learned to stand alone,
   and so will I.

7. Reality is the search for dreams to make life real.

8. Love has no past,
   for if it ends, it never was.
   Love has no future,
   for tomorrow's expectations leave it no room.

Love was not.
Love will not be.
Love is.

Lacks Flow

Am I to be
every man you ever thought of loving?

I find myself trying to flex muscles
I don't have and didn't need to have
in the yesterdays before I found you.

It's taken their lives to become what makes you smile.
Yet I try to be it all at once,
and forget I make you smile sometimes, too.

It frightens me that I need to be loved so much;
I'm willing to forsake my path
to find theirs
  that you've seemed to cross.
I keep forgetting
that I'm searching for nothing,
that I'm only waiting
for another to find that her path and mine are the same.
So it only makes sense
  to keep going.

I wish I could live what I write.

Neverminds

I held you last night
and I knew I could never hold you tight enough,
 and I suppose I got a little rough
 with you
 trying to do so anyway.

With my head on your shoulder
and you in my arms
I didn't want much
save your touch
and that I'd been given.

I didn't want words
 for they might have been wrong.

I didn't want time
 since it could only give me an end
 for a minute I didn't want to die.

I didn't want a memory
 like a key
 to have in my lonely times
to assure me
with transient solidarity
 that when, I next see you,
I can unlock your soul,
for I'd be forgetting

you never close it
to anyone.

I just wanted to hold you,
and walk a little further
and live another lifetime
in the walking.

Conversation

Last night,
I awoke from an open-eyed sleep
and beat back restless fears
with assurance that my spirit
will overcome
and live
 so long as I believe in it.
Last night, I spoke with God.

Thoughts That Keep Awake

...to sleep would make a yesterday of the time
    when we were close...

...I fear not knowing you well so much
    that I hesitate to reach to touch,
     so I might know you better...

All For Now

To mold myself from ideas
 of virtue and honesty.
Is as ridiculous as saying,
 "I know what I'm meant to be."
For if I make my life and play

and cast me in a role
the crowd who only watch the thing
will have as part my soul.

Thanksgiving Questions

Is it that I'm so bored by reality
  that I invent life to search for,
or is it that others are so bound by life
  that they refuse to seek reality?

Responsibilities #2

Sometimes I'd like to say, "I love you"
  and shun all I've said to you and myself.

I see you now in freedom
  and those words seem an able cage
  for preserving such beauty.

I won't say, "I love You,"
  but my mind hides every reason,
  and its only because I've not said it,
  that I won't.

Aftermath

Poets reach too hard.

I wish I could find a flower within me
  that would be an answer
  instead of myriad questions.

Title/First Thought: The Only Reward Received If We Accept Growing Old Is A Pungent Longing To Be Young

When I was a child, I knew what God looked like
and saw heaven in the sky
and knew hell was below me.

I believed in happy endings
and I felt what I felt
and didn't try to imprison my feelings
in cages called love and hate or sad and happy.

When I felt like singing I sang
and when the clouds looked like mountains
I said so without fear of those who'd call me trite.

Time was neither an ally nor enemy
but just another playground.

When I was a child, I was never too hurried
to watch a sunset.

And now I've head them say I'm a man.
I wonder if I've grown—
or just grown older.

Susan's

So if I say, "I love you,"
most likely its true.
But if our paths are one
 I cannot say.
And if they crossed for
 only that day
your smile I'll soon forget—
 but I'll keep the love of the time we met
 and were one.
And with our being done
 I'll go on to live with another
although it will be the same,
she'll just have another name,
and I'll love the love with her
 just as I loved the love with you.

Not Again

God I want to pick you,
to rip you from the ground,
and show you off as something new,
 a beauty I have found.

But I'll let you grow
  because I know what I want
  and you can't live on flowers very long.

Explanation

I marvel at your wisdom
 whoever made the thorn,
and am very thankful
He made you to be born
with beauty to make me want you
 and mystery to make me need you.

Spring

I'm afraid to smell spring's flower
 for I might kill the fruit of the fall,
 and then I'd be left with nothing at all
 to keep me in the winter times,
 and my rhymes
 might give up and grow cold,
 and I might give up and grow old.

So I sit in my spring
 and feel it a curious thing
 that when I found you
 I found so many questions
 and so much life.

December Showers

I walked home
as the world cried a guilty rain
and felt cold knowing you knew pain
 this day.
I needed words to say,
"I wish I'd gone for you."
But don't think the wish born of virtue.
It's built from selfishness,
for I'd have so much less
to trouble me
 were I in your place.

Early Spring

I'm not ready to be lonely again.
Winter collapsed too soon on me
as I climbed on it to try and see
 a spring that would follow.
Now all I have to show
Is desolate cold that tells me
 you were here, but aren't now.

Eyes Meet

Pardon me for staring
 but I really cannot tell
 if you will be my next love,
 or finally be my last—
if you will be my future,
 or a forgotten piece of past.

Questions #3

How many flowers were left without beauty
because there was no one there to see them?
Or were they beautiful, still?
Was the beauty in their being or in the will
 of someone who wished to worship them.

Nature is wondrous
and we should revere all we see.
But unfortunately it seems we don't see much
for by presuming to judge beauty
 we display our blindness.

Third Quarter

I know I can live without you
but I don't want to.
I can stand and watch the time float past
 and survive the cold in the shadows it casts
when it passes between you and me,
and builds an imprisoning wall, you see
 with you on your side
and me with you,
but on my side.

I know I can live
like this,
or at least stay alive
 if I must.

November

Could a flower be so eloquent
  to find the words to tell
how sorry I am for thoughts I thought
  when I didn't know you well?

Could a flower have such beauty
  to reflect to you your smile
or hold the wisdom to prophesize
  that we'll be friends a while?

But I can give only a flower
  whose message I can't understand
for only you will hear it
  when I place it in your hand.

Gold Rush

The deepness echoed words of darkness
  before I was bold to ask.
I fly cautiously into grayness
  as a prospector enters his task.
Almost sure, but not quite sure
  that this vein of gold could last.
Knowing well what the future could be,
  learning it from the past.

The treasure in your eyes, my love,
  is their mirror of what's me,
for the colors there are brighter—
  they show what I could be.

Crying

I love you for you have filled my void
with loneliness,
and the joy
of the hope
that you'll return.

Wasted

How sweet this music,
 were you to hear it.
How majestic this night,
 were you to see it.
How mighty this hand,
 were you to hold It.
How loved this life,
 were you to share it.

How real this pain alone.

What Now?

I'm afraid that you might be dying
 and my greatest wish,
since I don't believe in heaven,
 is that there is a God
and He made me a fool.

Crumpled Paper Philosophy

1. I was happy, but I forgot why,
     and while I looked for reasons, my happy died.

2. Friends seldom ask much of each other.
    Friends seldom have to ask.

3. I know I love you
    when the dusk is not
    the end of the day,
    but is instead
    the beginning of night.

4. Before I knew you I wondered why I am.
     when I hold you now, I wonder that I am.

5. When I say "I love You,"
    I'm not asking to slow your life down,
     so I can catch up to you and watch you smile.
    I'm not asking you to follow me,
     and I will clear your way.
    I'm just asking if you'll hold my hand
     as we go.

On A Bus

"Lord have mercy on us!"
I heard a man say.
It sure would be nice if He
 showed us some.
Wait a minute.
Maybe He is—
 showing us mercy, I mean.
If He is
I hope He doesn't stop,
 because if He did
 this world would really be screwed-up.

Unheard Songs

In my days when you're not here,
all the warmth and sun and blue,
and changing leaves and sunset hues,
make more distinct my missing you.
My days, it seems
are remembered dreams
on mornings when there's no one awake to hear them.

In my days when you're not here,
beauty is barbed with the anxious fear
those times without malice or rain
won't come again.
And I'd regret having wasted them,
for we didn't live them together.
And beauty isn't,
unless it's shared.

I'm aware as I write these words,
they'll remain like a song unheard,
without meaning or rhyme,
until the time
you make them real
by reading them.

Expendable Demands

Is the purpose to hunt for a purpose?
If not, then **give** me a reason
 for hanging around.
If the purpose is the being,
 then let me live and not ask why.
There are so many paths to take,
and all roads lead to death, right?
I don't even know if I have a choice.
Give me a way to go, damn it
Someone sell me god
for He seems to give direction, if you can believe.
Give me piece of mind
or contentment with myself, at least,
to slow my errant cascade.
Give me love
and make the searching easier, maybe.
Make the game less severe.
Lay your cards down
for the first few hands and teach me.
This is the first time I've played.
Give me a break.

Give me a minute to collect myself,
 and shut up.

War

How do you kill a cloud?
I can't really say,
but there must be a way.
If I die trying, my shroud
will be my flag, and I'll be proud
 to die for what they made me believe was right.
But now I'm alert inside this night
ordered to wait and be first to catch sight
of the haze that would steal the sunlight
that keeps my country free.

Far in the morning distance I see
the hazy cloud, my enemy.
From my sheltered home I raise
to send hungry lead into the haze.
I wait to hear the cries of pain,
but instead I hear shots again,
 and these weren't mine.

Now I find
that I'm listening to the birds last song,
and I feel something must be wrong,
for surely now there's more important things—
but my mind still listens to the birds that sings.

As I look now before me
not a haze but a man I see
and in his eyes
I see the lies
they told him die.
He and I now know the truth
and we see that our spirit of youth
was used to make us see an enemy
where a cloud of misunderstood ideas lay,
and we were made
to hate it.
We saw nothing else when it came
and we shot the cloud without shame.
Only this could satisfy our hate,
and it was too late
to see
only haze was between him and me.

The cloud didn't stop the shot from my gun,
it simply added the smoke from my weapon
and floated by,
leaving us to die,
 With my bullet in him
and his in me.

A Song For Jen, My Love

Not many words rhyme with Jennifer, you know.
So it's kind of hard for me to show
what I feel in a poem.
 And I roam
 through explanations
 hoping to find a gift pretty enough to give you.

You're old enough not to play with my love
if I give it to you.
you won't use is or break it
and then cry for something new.
But are you young enough still
to hear me say
that the love when I'm with you
is alive for that day
because you make me smile
when you smile?

Jenny, the love I give you
is a sunny day thing,
like a song that I sing
when you remind me
of the melody.
You can leave it or hear it or give it harmony.
But you mustn't fear it
for no bonds can it tie,

it's just drifting by,
and will fade to give way to another.

Correspondence #4

Because one and one don't equal one—
does this mean the ones are at fault?

Because the pieces don't fit
 does this make them guilty of some terrible crime?

You can't mourn a flower that never grew.

You can't worry over the collapse of a bridge
 that led nowhere, and brought nothing together.

God, that's easy to say when you're on the outside.
But it still hurts,
 doesn't it?
It's a uniqueness
that everyone shares
 in loneliness.
It hurts like hell.

Ona

I had been told of her.
Stories told in quiet times,
 almost in reverence,
grow now into warnings
 that give my mind no rest.
There is silence as I watch
the approaching storm.
Yet, I hear the most beautiful threats
tug at my freedom,
 and I imagine
 she calls to me.
I feel her challenge to embrace
and become blind to all but her.

But I am afraid.
Not that I would lose my life in her,
but that she would pass.
 Imprisoning me in a world
that could only be
 as it was before.

Redbird

Do you stay redbird just to sing,
and bare a dead autumn on your wing,
so perhaps a world thinking winter's come
will see you and believe the warmth's not done?

Redbird, it's too hard your way.
If you'd only cry with us today,
you'd cry for a spring that's not yet come,
and not give tears to a dead autumn.

Warmth and flowers always go
only by understanding this can you know
the happiness of their return.
I promise you'll learn
if you'll stop smiling when you feel pain,
you can feel joy when it comes again,
to make you smile.

Don't make us see summer when you fly.
If you try to do that you're likely to die
 in the cold,
and so will part of me.

As You Pass By

Desire as elusive
 as ambition,
yet real enough
to trigger my next breath.
Evidence that my pulse
resonates with a smile.
Desire, whose tip
 so honed
that it pierces my soul effortlessly,
but with a barb so severe
 it promises to tear apart
 tomorrow.

Hiding the Elephant

As secret as the sunrise,
 as subtle as the light,
I struggle with the feelings—
I fear I'll lose the fight.

Then a heartbeat later,
I finally do recall
the moments you saw me seeing you
 and I know you know it all.

Lost and Found

When our moment passes,
 if we never touch,
tomorrow's promise
 won't seem so much.

When our moment passes,
 if we never dance,
I'll forever regret
 not taking the chance.

When our moment passes,
if we've never kissed,
I won't soon forget
the opportunities missed.

But if I look back
on our time that is through,
I couldn't go on
if I never knew you.

Finally, About You

This day, not another, you chose to die
and I can't escape the question "why?'
As if understanding could heal
the aching emptiness that I feel.

Could your answers have come
 in a moments delay,
rising up with the sunrise
 the following day.
Had the darkness become so true,
death was the only escape from you?

Words become whispers, images fade,
 lives remain measured by friendships made.
I choose today to say goodbye,
and leave for you the reasons why.

Isolated

The fearful man believes there is no God.
The lonely man believes God doesn't listen to his prayers.
The religious man believes God will answer his prayers.
The spiritual man believes God answers his prayer,
 and the answer is often "no."

Look Closely

Let me scrutinize my blessings enough
 to find humility,
 and my burdens enough
to find gratitude.

Love Becomes

Love isn't found—
 love becomes.

To encourage is love,
 to yield is love.

To teach is love,
 to learn is love.

To rejoice is love,
 to mourn is love.

To share is love.

For love to become a noun,
 it must live as a verb.

By Way Of Explanation, In Rhyme

I tried to recall my first thought,
but came to understand,
it was my feelings that brought
 a life to what is me.
It seems I was cast in an endless sea,
when I was born and became aware,
drifting in a life ring not concerned where.
Floating was all I had to do,
and the sea felt calm, the currents few.

But voices carried across the endless sea,
that disrupted my childhood reverie,
and told me I had places to go.
My awakening created a boat I could row
and with work I had motion.
I commanded my boat—a powerful notion.

I pulled my boat through the endless sea,
one hand on each oar, but the rudder stayed free.
Still, I learned of and reached many memorable places,
and friendships were made with encountered new faces.

But the waves in my path seemed no longer still,
and with effort I enlarged my boat until
no wave could wash over the side.
But rowing grew harder with arms stretched so wide.

Soon a tempest raged and tried to swallow me.
I despaired at how long and wide my boat must be
to stay above the ocean's floor.
I gave up trying to reach both oars
 and floundered.

It was then you arrived to rescue me,
a miraculous meeting on our endless sea.
You came aboard and unafraid of the weather
showed we could each, at an oar, pull together
to make headway to ride the storm out.
And soon it grew quiet, but still, I had doubt.
"With you at your oar and me pulling mine
the rudder is unmanned, we can't keep a straight line."

It was then that you taught me what I now live as true.
Our rudder is unmanned and we are but crew,
for God masters the tiller, our course is his will,
and this journey together our lives will fill.
So now our task remains to row
and accept the truth that we can't know,
 our shared destiny.
Such truth gives serenity.

0-595-26918-4